AVICENNA

Prince of Physicians

Written by
Reza Shah-Kazemi
&
Illustrated by
Fatima Zahra Hassan

HOOD HOOD BOOKS

Hood Hood Books
46 Clabon Mews
London SW1X OEH

Tel: 44 171 5847878
Fax: 44 171 2250386

British Library Cataloguing–in–Publication Data
A catalogue record for this book is available from the British Library

ISBN 1 900251 23 X

Origination: Fine Line Graphics-London
Printed by IPH, Egypt

AVICENNA

✳

Many may be clever, but few are truly wise
For wisdom shows you things that are hidden from men's eyes.
Avicenna was given wisdom before he came of age
And proved while still a beardless youth that he was already a great sage.

In the year 980, in a small village near Bukhara in the country now called Uzbekistan, a baby boy was born whose mind was going to become like a brilliant star that illuminates everything around it. "Prince of Physicians", "Leader of the Wise", "Proof of God": these and many other titles were showered on Avicenna. In the history of the world there have been great philosophers, great doctors, great scientists and great writers: but Avicenna was all of these things at the same time. What is even more astounding is that he said he had learnt everything he knew by the time he was eighteen years old! If that is hard to believe, then listen to the story of the infant Avicenna and his mother's golden necklace...

When he was just three months old, Avicenna's mother lay him in a wicker cot in the garden of the family home. The wicker cot had a hood over the baby's head to keep the flies from pestering him; as it was wicker it was full of small holes, holes that were big enough to let the air in, but small enough to keep the flies out. Now the time for prayer came along, and Avicenna's mother went to the pool to wash herself; she took off her golden necklace and hung it carefully on the branch of a nearby tree. She said her prayers and forgot all about the necklace. After a few days, she realised that her necklace was missing and set about looking for it with her husband and the whole household; but to no avail: it could only have been stolen, they all concluded, sadly.

Three years passed, and Avicenna was sitting with his mother and a friend in the very same garden, when the necklace was mentioned:"Oh, it was such a beautiful necklace," his mother sighed, "I would give anything to have it back again; but this is just wishful thinking – it's gone forever."

"No it hasn't, mother," little Avicenna piped up, "I know where it is." In disbelief, but charmed by her little boy's gallant attempt at cheering her up, she asked him:

"Well, my son, tell us, where is it?"

"It's over there, hanging on the branch of that tree near the pool. You put it there one day, a long time ago, when the sky was full of holes!"

His mother then went and, sure enough, there was her necklace, exactly where Avicenna said it was. And she suddenly remembered the day she had laid him in the wicker cot with the hood: for the little baby, the sky really was full of holes – but how on earth could he have remembered?

✸

By this time, though, Avicenna's parents knew that their little boy was no ordinary child: he was a child-prodigy, a genius in the making. He continued to amaze all who came to visit the family, with his sharp wit, his good manners, his extraordinary words, but most of all, the speed with which he learnt whatever he was taught. At the age of five, his father moved to Bukhara, a thriving centre of Muslim culture and learning; there, he was able to provide Avicenna with the best teachers in the land.

By the time he was ten, Avicenna had mastered not only his mother tongue, which was Persian, but also the Arabic language; he had learnt the Holy Qur'an by heart, and had studied and memorised numerous works of literature. All his teachers confessed that they had never seen anything like it:

"Let this boy study, and don't force him to do anything else," they all told his father, "because he truly is destined to become one of the most learned men in all the world."

"By the grace of God," replied his father, who took to heart their advice.

Avicenna had an unquenchable thirst for knowledge; he studied all the sciences of the day: mathematics and biology, literature and history, astronomy and medicine. He not only studied medicine, but even started, while still in his teens, to practise it, curing people around him of their diseases. Indeed, his fame as a healer spread so far and wide that learned doctors came from distant lands to consult him, learn from him, and gaze in wonder at this youth of sixteen who surpassed them in learning.

It was at this time that the Prince of Bukhara fell seriously ill; and none of the physicians at the royal court could cure him. The King was worried that his son might soon die, and consulted his advisers. Now one of them had heard that in the city there lived a great physician by the name of Avicenna, who could perform marvels. The King ordered his courtiers to go immediately to this great physician, offer him the finest gifts, and request him to come to the palace to treat the sick prince.

The courtiers came, after a long search, to the house of Avicenna, and asked his mother:

"Where is the one named Avicenna? We have come on urgent business from the King himself."

"He's playing in the garden," she replied, to their astonishment. "Have we been tricked?" they wondered to themselves, "how could the greatest physician in the land be playing in the garden?"

They went to the garden, however, to see for themselves; and they found the youth up a walnut tree, picking nuts.

"Are you really Avicenna?" they asked him, incredulously.

"I am," he replied.

"Well, the King has said to us: 'go and find Avicenna and bring him to me, from wherever you may find him on this earth.'"

"Go back to the King," Avicenna replied, "and tell him that you cannot bring Avicenna back because you did not find him anywhere on earth, but up in the sky, on the branch of a tree!"

Bemused and humiliated, the courtiers returned to the royal court and told the King what had taken place. There happened to be present in the court a physician who had attended one of Avicenna's classes on medicine. He laughed heartily after hearing the story and said:

"He may be a child in appearance but do not be fooled: he really is the greatest physician in the land."

Avicenna was again requested to come and treat the prince; this he did, and the prince soon regained full health. The King, overwhelmed with gratitude, said that he would grant Avicenna anything he wanted, as a reward for saving the prince's life.

"There is only one thing I would like, oh King," replied Avicenna, "and that is to be able to come and read all the books in the palace library."

This wish was granted; and Avicenna was now able to delve deeply into the accumulated knowledge and sciences of the ages. He studied not only the great works of Muslims but also the books of the Greeks, the Persians, the Egyptians, even the ancient

Mesopotamians! He thus became a master of almost all the different philosophies and sciences of the world. After he had learnt all he could from this library, he set off on many journeys to other great cities, such as Isfahan and Hamadan in Persia, in search of knowledge.

Like all the great Islamic thinkers, Avicenna was deeply religious. He used to pray much and he always used to thank God whenever he was able to solve a problem or cure a sick person. He wrote once that whenever he came across a question that he could not understand, he would pray to God to show him the solution. Then he would go home and sleep, and in his dreams he would see the answer to the problem. Sometimes he would get up immediately, and write a whole book on the question, even if it was in the middle of the night!

Now Avicenna was not only a great physician and a philosopher: he was also very wise. He used his wisdom when treating sick people; that is why he was called a *hakim*, which means one who is both a wise man and a doctor at the same time.

Most of the time Avicenna treated his patients with carefully selected medicines, but at other times he would use unconventional methods. This is because, through his wisdom, he came to see the real – often hidden – causes of illness. One such case involved another Prince in Persia. He had a sickness that first made him very thin, and finally affected his brain: the poor boy became certain that he was a cow, and pleaded to be killed by the butcher! Everyone tried to convince him that he was not a cow, but a human being, but the only reply they got from him was a loud MOOO!

The King and Queen were naturally horrified at their son's madness and did what they could to bring the best doctors to court; but to no avail, for the boy would neither eat any food nor take any of the prescribed medicine. Finally, Avicenna's name was mentioned to the King, who was now so desperate that he immediately sent a message to Avicenna, begging him to come and cure his son. When he arrived at the palace and saw the state of the Prince, Avicenna said: "I shall treat the boy, but on one condition: that you all follow my instructions to the letter." The King and the whole court agreed.

Avicenna proceeded to set up a butcher's shop in the court-yard of the palace, and he up himself as a butcher, brandishing a long sharp knife in each hand: "Bring the Prince to me," he ordered, much to the terror of all present: but they had promised

to do whatever he said, so they had no choice. In came the Prince, mooing on his bed, which was carried into the courtyard by his attendants

"Bring me that cow," said Avicenna, pointing to the Prince, "I shall slaughter it now, because we need a lot of meat today." At this, the prince mooed loudly, delighted that at last someone believed that he was a cow. Avicenna approached the Prince, carving knife in hand, and was about to cut the boy's throat when suddenly he said:

"No, this cow won't do, she's far too thin! We will get hardly any meat out of her. Take her away, feed her for a month until she's nice and fat, and then bring her back to me to be slaughtered."

The Prince bellowed in dismay, longing to be slaughtered there and then. He was taken back to his room, where Avicenna gave orders for him to be offered large dishes of nutritious food. He so wanted to be fattened for the slaughter that the Prince ate whatever was put in front of him, much to the astonished delight of his parents, the King and Queen. It was only now, once the boy was eating again, that Avicenna resorted to normal medicine: he chose the remedies that he thought the boy needed, and carefully mixed them into the dishes that the Prince gobbled up unquestioningly. To the relief and joy of all, the Prince gradually regained his strength, his mind returned to normal, and his life as a cow was now just like a funny dream from which he had, thankfully, woken up!

❋

Avicenna wrote many, many books on subjects as diverse as medicine and mathematics, geology and philosophy, zoology and physics, to name just a few. He also wrote the longest encyclopaedia of knowledge ever written by one man alone; it was called Al-Shifa which means "The Remedy".

His most famous book, however, was the "The Canon", a huge book on medicine that was used as a text-book for hundreds of years, not only in the Islamic world, but also in Europe, where Avicenna was always being quoted as the authority on medicine. In this book there are many chapters on different illnesses and their cures; there is even a chapter on "Love" – its symptoms and how to treat them. Here is one interesting case that was brought to Avicenna.

A young man, Ali, had suddenly and without any reason fallen ill; whatever medicines he was given only made him worse. He was finally brought to Avicenna, who asked to be left alone with Ali. With his finger on Ali's pulse, Avicenna asked him a series of questions. When asked where he lived, Ali's pulse suddenly jumped.

"What places do you visit?" Avicenna asked.

"The mosque, the bazaar, the baker..." came the reply; but at the mention of the baker, Ali's pulse started racing.

"Tell me more about the baker," said Avicenna.

"Well, he's a good friend of mine, I see him quite regularly, in fact I was invited to his house for dinner some time ago..." Avicenna noticed that at the mention of the word "dinner", Ali's pulse again accelerated.

"What happened at that dinner?" he asked him.

"We had excellent food cooked by his wife and then some lovely *halwa* from his bakery. And after dinner his sister came into the dining room..." Avicenna now discovered what he was looking for: no sooner had the word "sister" been mentioned than Ali's heart started pounding quite uncontrollably. The poor young man was simply love-sick!

Avicenna then went to Ali's parents and told them that there was only one thing that could cure their son: marriage to the baker's sister! They were amazed at this diagnosis, but nonetheless arranged the marriage; and, sure enough, within a few days Ali was restored to full health.

Avicenna travelled much from city to city, but he never stopped teaching and writing: even when accompanying a king on the way to a battle he would dictate a book to his secretary on horseback! He was employed by different princes and kings, mostly as court physician or teacher; but he even became a vizier at the court of one king, Shams al-Dawlah of Hamadan. His longest stay in any one place was at the royal court of King Ala' al-Dawlah in Isfahan; in the fifteen years that Avicenna lived there it became a thriving centre of learning and culture. Avicenna wrote many of his books there and also built an observatory for the study of the stars.

When Avicenna was at the height of his fame, one of his most devoted pupils said to him:

"Oh master! You are such a great genius, why don't you declare yourself to be a prophet? So many people believe in you and do whatever you tell them; your new religion would surely have many followers, you would become rich and powerful, and I would be your first faithful servant!"

Avicenna simply replied that he would think about it. For the rest of the day nothing was said about the subject. They both worked very hard in the library until late into the evening. Then, the thoroughly exhausted pupil asked if he could go to sleep. Avicenna gave him permission, and before long the youth was snoring, sound asleep. Now it was a very cold night, in the middle of winter, and the pool in the garden was frozen over. After some hours, Avicenna decided that the time had come to teach the young man the difference between a prophet and a genius.

"Wake up, wake up!" he shouted at his pupil.

Irritated at being so rudely woken, but doing his best to control his anger, the pupil said, "What is it? What's the matter?"

"I'm thirsty," replied Avicenna quite calmly, "can you get me a glass of water?"

At this the young man exploded: "You woke me up just for a glass of water! Can't you get it yourself?"

"Of course, I'm terribly sorry, please go back to sleep ..." said Avicenna.

A few hours later, when the darkness of night was just beginning to yield to the first glimmerings of dawn, the pupil woke up to say his morning prayers; he went out into the garden, broke the ice over the pool, made his ablutions with freezing water, and said his prayers. After the prayers he asked Avicenna whether he had given any further thought to his suggestion of the previous day. Avicenna laughed and said:

"Do you remember what happened when I asked you last night for a glass of water?"

"Yes," the pupil replied, blushing with embarassment.

"Well, what kind of a prophet can I be, when you cannot even get up to give me a glass of water? But you get up, while it's still dark in the freezing cold, to wash with icy water and then pray – all this you do because of the teachings of a man called Muhammad who died 400 years ago."

Avicenna had made his point well: the young man realised that a prophet's authority comes from God, and that is why he is obeyed by millions of people all over the world and for hundreds and thousands of years; but a genius is just an ordinary man, a cut above the average, it is true, but as different from a prophet as a pebble is from a diamond.

Avicenna passed away at the age of 53; he died of colic, a disease on which he had written a famous treatise. And that was the last lesson he taught his students: however much you may uncover the mysteries of God's creation, you must never forget that all your knowledge, along with your very life and your death - all of this is in the hands of God. Perhaps it was this lesson that Avicenna had in mind when he said that he had learnt everything by the time he was eighteen; for whoever understands this lesson is truly wise, however old or young they may be.

HEROES FROM THE EAST